RAVENOUS VULTURES

by Bryan Langdo

Minneapolis, Minnesota

Credits
Cover and title page, © Henk Bogaard/Shutterstock and © John Twynam/iStock; 5, © stefanov764/Adobe Stock Images; 6, © Francesco De Marco/Adobe Stock Images; 6–7, © Sebek/Adobe Stock Images; 8, © Lawrence Lee Derge/Shutterstock; 9, © Creative Nature/Adobe Stock Images; 10, © Irfan Photographer786/Shutterstock; 11, © Ian Dyball/Shutterstock; 12–13, © Keith/Adobe Stock Images; 15, © Angelika/iStock; 17, © adammajor/Adobe Stock Images; 18–19, © Rafaruizfoto/Wirestock Creators/Adobe Stock Images; 20, © imageBROKER/Juergen Kosten/Getty Images; 21, © Ishor gurung/Shutterstock; 22TR, © James/Adobe Stock Images; 22ML, © John/Adobe Stock Images; 22BR, © Dr Ajay Kumar Singh/Adobe Stock Images; 23, © Harry Collins/Adobe Stock Images

Bearport Publishing Company Product Development Team
Publisher: Jen Jenson; Director of Product Development: Spencer Brinker; Editorial Director: Allison Juda; Editor: Cole Nelson; Editor: Tiana Tran; Production Editor: Naomi Reich; Art Director: Kim Jones; Designer: Kayla Eggert; Designer: Steve Scheluchin; Production Specialist: Owen Hamlin

Statement on Usage of Generative Artificial Intelligence
Bearport Publishing remains committed to publishing high-quality nonfiction books. Therefore, we restrict the use of generative AI to ensure accuracy of all text and visual components pertaining to a book's subject. See BearportPublishing.com for details.

Library of Congress Cataloging-in-Publication Data is available at www.loc.gov or upon request from the publisher.

ISBN 979-8-89577-060-3 (hardcover)
ISBN: 979-8-89577-177-8 (ebook)

Copyright © 2026 Bearport Publishing Company. All rights reserved. No part of this publication may be reproduced in whole or in part, stored in any retrieval system, or transmitted in any form or by any means, electronic, mechanical, photocopying, recording, or otherwise, without written permission from the publisher. Bearport Publishing is a division of FlutterBee Education Group.

For more information, write to Bearport Publishing, 3500 American Blvd W, Suite 150, Bloomington, MN 55431.

CONTENTS

The Smell of Death............ 4
Hungry Raptors 6
Around the World............. 8
Tireless Flyers................ 10
On the Lookout.............. 12
A Shared Meal............... 14
Feeding Time 16
Starting a Family............. 18
Learning to Eat 20

Meet the Birds 22
Glossary 23
Index 24
Read More 24
Learn More Online............. 24
About the Author.............. 24

THE SMELL OF DEATH

A bird with wide wings soars high in the sky. Suddenly, it notices something nasty—the smell of death! An animal's body is beginning to rot in a hot, sunny field. The large bird follows the smell and lands next to the **carcass**. It uses its sharp beak to rip into the flesh. This hungry bird is a **raptor** called a vulture.

> Vultures poop and pee on their own legs! They do this to cool off and protect themselves from harmful **bacteria** in their rotting meals.

HUNGRY RAPTORS

Raptors are also known as birds of prey. As **apex predators**, these fierce creatures hunt other animals without being hunted themselves. Sharp talons and beaks allow these birds to tear apart flesh. Most raptors are highly skilled hunters but not vultures. These birds of prey almost never hunt live animals. Instead, they are **scavengers**, preferring to chow down on **carrion**, or dead meat.

Most vultures have bald heads, which help them stay clean as they stick their heads into carcasses.

Owls are also raptors.

AROUND THE WORLD

Vultures live in fields, forests, and deserts on every continent except Australia and Antarctica. These birds are divided into two main groups. New World vultures live in North and South America while Old World vultures can be found in Africa, Asia, and Europe. Although they look alike, the groups are not closely related to each other.

New World vultures have long toes that help them walk on the ground.

White-backed vultures are one kind of Old World vulture.

TIRELESS FLYERS

Vultures are large birds. The smallest **species** has a **wingspan** of 5 feet (1.5 m), and the largest can be nearly 10 ft. (3 m) from wing tip to wing tip. These wide wings let the birds soar miles above the ground for hours at a time. As the scavengers glide in circles, they look for signs of death below.

Vultures are some of the world's largest flying birds.

Some vultures can fly as far as 200 miles (322 km) in one day.

ON THE LOOKOUT

Some vultures have an amazing sense of smell. They can detect a dead mouse from up to 1 mile (1.6 km) away! But most of these raptors use their keen eyesight to find food. They look for carrion while also keeping an eye on other vultures. If one vulture spots a dead animal and lands, others quickly notice and follow.

By eating dead animals, vultures help stop diseases from spreading.

A SHARED MEAL

When vultures gather, the largest eat first while the smaller ones wait. But even the biggest birds back off when predators, such as hyenas, come along. They wait nearby because they probably won't be attacked. Predators know vultures are covered in bacteria that can make them sick if they take a bite.

If a predator gets too close, some vultures vomit at the creature to scare it away.

FEEDING TIME

Vultures often go a long time between eating. So, when they do find a good meal, they stuff themselves as much as they can. They usually start with the soft parts of a carcass, such as the tongue, eyeballs, and rear end. A special pouch in their throats lets vultures store some of this food for later.

> Powerful acids in a vulture's stomach can break down the bones of dead animals.

The pouch in a vulture's neck that is use to store food is called a crop.

Crop

STARTING A FAMILY

Vultures usually **mate** for life. Old World vultures make nests on cliffs or in trees. New World vultures don't make nests. These birds settle down somewhere hidden, such as inside a cave or abandoned building. The **female** vulture lays one or two eggs. Then, she and her partner take turns **incubating** them. The eggs hatch into baby chicks up to 68 days later.

Some Old World vultures will take over nests left by other birds, such as hawks.

LEARNING TO EAT

Vulture parents bring food back to their young. At first, they **regurgitate** the meat right into the chicks' mouths. As the birds grow older, the parents spit up nearby and let the children pick it up themselves. After two to three months, the young terrors are ready to take flight. Soon, they head off to live on their own.

Some vultures can live for up to 50 years in the wild.

A young Egyptian vulture taking off

MEET THE BIRDS

There are about 22 species of vultures. Let's take a look at some of them!

Turkey Vulture
Turkey vultures have the strongest sense of smell of any vulture. This allows them to sniff out a carcass that is more than a mile away. These are the most common vultures in the United States.

Andean Condor
With a wingspan of 10 ft. (3 m), the Andean condor is the largest vulture species. These raptors live in the Andes Mountains. They can glide on air currents for up to 100 miles (160 km) without flapping their wings.

Rüppell's Griffon Vulture
Rüppell's griffon vultures live across central Africa. While searching for food, this vulture can fly as high as 7 miles (11 km) and stay in the air for as long as 7 hours. Its stomach acid is so powerful that it can even eat rotting or diseased meat!

GLOSSARY

apex predators animals that hunt without being hunted by any other animals

bacteria tiny organisms that can cause disease

carcass the body of a dead animal

carrion flesh that is dead and rotting

female a vulture that can lay eggs

incubating sitting on eggs to keep them warm until they hatch

mate to come together to have young

raptor a large, strong bird with a hooked beak and large talons that eats mostly meat

regurgitate to throw up food that is partly digested

scavengers animals that look for and eat dead things

species groups that animals are divided into, according to similar characteristics

wingspan the distance between the tips of a bird's wings

23

INDEX

apex predators 6
bacteria 4, 14
beak 4, 6
carcass 4, 6, 16, 22
carrion 6, 12
chicks 18, 20
eyesight 12
nests 18–19
New World vultures 8, 18
Old World vultures 8–9, 18–19
raptor 4, 6–7, 12, 22
scavengers 6, 10
wingspan 10, 22

READ MORE

Grack, Rachel. *California Condors (Animals at Risk).* Minneapolis: Bellwether Media, 2024.

Markle, Sandra. *Vultures: Nature's Cleanup Crew (Animal Scavengers in Action).* Minneapolis: Lerner Publications, 2024.

Riggs, Kate. *Vultures (Amazing Animals).* Mankato, MN: Creative Education, 2023.

LEARN MORE ONLINE

1. Go to **FactSurfer.com** or scan the QR code below.
2. Enter "**Ravenous Vultures**" into the search box.
3. Click on the cover of this book to see a list of websites.

ABOUT THE AUTHOR

Bryan Langdo has written more than 20 books for children and illustrated plenty of others. He lives in New Jersey with his wife, two kids, three dogs, and three cats.